D0816609

NO LONGER PROPERTY
OF ANYTHINK
RANGEVIEW LIBRARY
DISTRICT

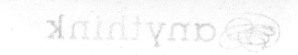

Seasons of the Boreal Forest Biome

Written by
Shirley Duke

Rourke
Educational Media

rourkeeducationalmedia.com

Scan for Related Titles
and Teacher Resources

© 2014 Rourke Educational Media

All rights reserved. No part of this book may be reproduced or utilized in any form or by any means, electronic or mechanical including photocopying, recording, or by any information storage and retrieval system without permission in writing from the publisher.

www.rourkeeducationalmedia.com

PHOTO CREDITS: Cover: Peter Wey; Title page photo © Elliotte Rusty Harold; © Becky Sheridan; page 4 notebook © PixelEmbargo; pine cone © stieberszabolcs; page 5 © evarin20; page 6 © NancyS; page 7 © scattoselvaggio; page 8 © Gerald A. DeBoer; page 9 © Lori Labrecque; page 10 © Tom Reichner; page 11 © Eric Wang; page 12/13 © Luca Villanova; page 12 inset photo © Galyna Andrushko, page 13 inset photo © Imfoto; page 14 © Pictureguy; page 15 © Steve Oehlenschlager; page 15 inset photo © via; page 16 © Chris Hill; page 17 © Volodymyr Burdiak, page 17 inset photo © Tom linster; page 19 © TTphoto; page 20 © Dasha Rosato; page 21 © Juriah Mosin

Edited by Jill Sherman

Cover design by Renee Brady
Interior design by Nicola Stratford bdpublishing.com

Library of Congress PCN Data

Seasons of the Boreal Forest Biome / Shirley Duke
(Biomes)
ISBN 978-1-62169-896-8 (hard cover)
ISBN 978-1-62169-791-6 (soft cover)
ISBN 978-1-62717-003-1 (e-Book)
Library of Congress Control Number: 2013936812

Also Available as:

Rourke Educational Media
Printed in the United States of America,
North Mankato, Minnesota

rourkeeducationalmedia.com
customerservice@rourkeeducationalmedia.com • PO Box 643328 Vero Beach, Florida 32964

Table of Contents

Needles and Cones

Boreal forests form the largest land biome. They ring northern Canada and Russia to the **tundra**.

Boreal Forests have:

✓ Six months of winter
✓ Lots of snow
✓ Short summers
✓ Trees with needles
✓ Lakes

Boreal Forest

Trees with needles in place of leaves fill boreal forests. These trees make cones that grow seeds inside. **Scales** on the cones open as they grow. The seeds fall out. Wind or animals spread them.

Cones stay tightly closed while growing. When the seeds inside are ready, the green cone turns brown, the scales separate, and the seeds fall out.

Seasons of Change

Winter lasts six months in the boreal forest. The cold brings heavy snow. Some animals sleep away the winter.

The Arctic ground squirrel has a beige and tan coat with a white-spotted back.

Other animals leave for warmer lands. Furry **mammals** like lynx and wolves hunt their food in the snow.

Lynx

Spring brings the birds back.

Boreal
songbird

Young are born.

Wolf

Summers are short in boreal forests. The air is humid.

Moose escape the heat and biting bugs in lakes.

Summer is a time for feasting and growing.

Grizzly bear

11

In the crisp fall, the green needles of the **conifer** trees, like spruces, firs, and pines, stay on their branches. Cones protect the growing seeds.

Animals, like grizzly bears, prepare for winter hibernation. They must eat more to store energy for their long winter nap.

Boreal forests also have some trees with leaves. In the fall, the leaves change colors and fall off the trees.

The leaves of aspens and alders turn yellow in fall and then fall off. Their broad leaves grow back in spring.

Life Among the Trees

Birds and mammals live in the boreal forest. Jays and nuthatches feed on seeds.

Great gray owls and ruffed grouse live in boreal forests year round.

The gray jay builds its nest in conifer trees.

Owls listen carefully and then fly in silence to catch a mouse or rabbit under the snow.

Grouse grow a skin-like fringe on each side of their toes to help them walk on the snow.

Garter snakes and wood frogs hunt small animals and insects on the ground.

The bodies of wood frogs freeze during winter. They thaw in spring and come back to life.

Wolves, lynx, and foxes hunt mammals in the forests. All year round, the boreal forest is a busy place.

Hares turn white to better hide in the winter snow.

Wolves must work hard to find food in the winter months.

Future of
the Boreal Forest

Forests are needed by people, animals, and plants. But, people cut down trees for lumber. It takes many years for trees to grow back. Animals lose their homes. Pollution harms the animals and plants.

Fewer trees mean more **carbon** stays in the air. Carbon holds heat in the air. The warming **climate** in boreal forests changes the kinds of trees that grow there.

People must use the forests in a way that also protects them. Protecting the forest gives animals homes. Replanting trees can renew forests.

To reduce air pollution, ride a bike and drive less.

Write letters to groups that help save our forests. Tell them you think forests are important. Help keep boreal forests safe.

You Can Help
Protect Forests:

✓ Use fewer paper products made from trees.
✓ Recycle paper.
✓ Pick up your trash from your forest visits.
✓ Plant a tree by your home.
✓ Reduce air pollution by walking instead of driving.

Study Like a Scientist
Study Like a Squirrel

1. Get a pine cone. Are the scales open or closed?

2. Pull apart some scales and remove them.

3. Check for any seeds that may still be inside. What do they look like?

The papery seeds birds and squirrels eat hide between the scales.

Glossary

boreal forests (BOR-ee-uhl FOR-ists): a northern biome made of cone bearing trees

carbon (KAHR-buhn): a material found in living things and in the air

climate (KLYE-mit): the weather in a place over time

conifer (KAH-nuh-fur): tree with needles that makes cones with seeds in them

mammals (MAM-uhlz): warm-blooded animals with hair or fur that feed their young from the mother's milk

scales (SKALZ): the small, dark pieces that join in the center of a pine cone and hold the seeds

tundra (TUHN-druh): bare land in the far north with a layer of ice under the ground all year

Index

Websites

www.incredibleworld.ca/kidscan/kidscan02

www.wildernessclassroom.com/students/archives/boreal_forest_
library/index.html

education.nationalgeographic.com/education/encyclopedia/
taiga/?ar_a=1

About the Author

Shirley Duke has written many books about science. She lives in Texas and New Mexico and loves the different seasons in each place. She likes the alpine forests of New Mexico, which are very much like boreal forests. The pines sway and hum when the wind blows.

Meet The Author!
www.meetREMauthors.com